Cymbalist Poems
Selected 1965-1977

by

Jean-Thomas Cullen

This poetry volume contains a special new 2016 Preface introducing the author's poetic, youthful novel written at 27, lost 40 years, first published in 2016, titled On Saint Ronan Street. Its hero, a young poet in a New England college town, has a passionate affair with a beautiful young married woman (faculty wife). The 2016 edition contains eleven poems from this selection. More info at 2016 Preface.

Clocktower Books
San Diego, California

Published by Clocktower Books, San Diego, 2016. Please note added new Preface in 2016. Used some of the poems in the novel *On Saint Ronan Street*.

Quote from introduction & dedication of 1980 collection **Pauses**:

> "As we heard that cry,
> And turned our eyes then
> To the moon-drunk skies of Boston,
> Knowing only that we were young,
> And drunk,
> And twenty,
> And that the power of mighty poetry
> Was within us,
> And the glory of the great earth
> Lay before us —
> Because we were young and drunk and twenty
> And could never die!" — Thomas Wolfe

* (*A Stone, A Leaf, A Door, Poems by Thomas Wolfe*, Selected and Arranged in Verse by John S. Barnes, Charles Scribner's Sons, New York, 1945)

Illustration: *Jephtha's Daughter*, Gustave Doré, 1865. Photo p26 Wilbur Cross Hall courtesy University of Connecticut. Yale arch iStockphoto. All other photos property of Jean-Thomas Cullen. Title page photo: Blankenberge, Belgium circa 1955

Cymbalist Poems
Selected 1965-1977

Companion Volume
("27" Novel titled <u>*On Saint Ronan Street*</u>)
Matches this Poetry Volume

(See the New 2016 Preface about My "27")

Luxembourg

CONTENTS

Luxembourg

CONTENTS

Luxembourg. Unbearable.

NEW 2016 PREFACE: MY "27"

TWIN COMPANION BOOKS: This new preface introduces both my "27" collection of poetry (*Cymbalist Poems*) and my "27" novel (*On Saint Ronan Street*).

The term "27" started as an innocent handle in 2016 between me and my editor—an internal code, shorthand for my novel written at age 27. Coincidentally, twenty-seven is the mythological age when many brilliant young rock stars have died (a long list, from Jimi Hendrix and Janis Joplin and Jim Morrison to Amy Winehouse and many more). I didn't die, but stopped writing lyrical poetry and turned my lyricism into tilling rich soil for many prose novels that came after the "27."

These two books belong together as a pair of snapshots, like book ends, from a lost age in my life, long ago. I am just fully realizing this now—age 66, forty years later—near winter's door. In a moment, I will tell you the special, wonderful insight that made the intersection work and the connection click.

I can only summarize the wonder of this intersection for lack of space in this brief preface. I hope to provide more info soon at my personal writer website & canoodle www.sharpwriter.com. It's an interesting tale, and I am a story teller. The intersection of these two books became clear to me only in 2016. In 1980, I had published a collection of my favorite poems. By then I had also written and shelved the manuscript (Jon + Merile) of the amazing novel I am just now publishing forty years later. Only upon completing polish & revisions in 2016 did I begin to see how critically interlinked these two books really have been—both then (1976) and now (2016).

I stopped writing poetry around age 27.

(I had by then written several novels; I would consider my "27" to be my first really adult novel, although maybe today it would be a New Adult novel, written by a 27 year old reflecting back on a lost past life at age 23.)

I had been writing poetry most of my life, was a published poet by age 18, took away a Literature degree (English, German, Classics, History) at the University of Connecticut, and was able to type up a collection of several hundred poems by age 23. I salvaged those 400+ poems from a cardboard box into which I used to throw scraps of paper on which I wrote poems at all sorts of odd moments (restaurants, bars, guard jobs, you name it) over many years. I typed all the poems into a single volume while working as a security guard in the brutally industrial setting of a gas and power station in New Haven Harbor, and I still have that collection with me.

Readers of my "27" novel will be reminded of the author at various odd moments. Some of the romantic entanglements, drinking buddies, Victorian apartments, moths, typing, minimum wage jobs, neo-Gothic (faux, neo-Gothoid?) Ivy League buildings, and what not are all carved from the burl and grain of my real oak and life back then. A certain incessant playfulness of language is part of that special fertilizer the poet brings in nurturing sacks to the task of writing prose; sometimes too rich a mix; and certainly there is much in my "27" novel because I was still a working, thinking, emoting poet at the time.

The novel remained a dusty manuscript needing final edits over forty years, until today I am just finishing rewrites in February 2016 at age 66. The first marvel about this novel is how effective and poetic the novel has struck me and other early readers in 2016. It was a marvelous first draft, needing some polish, but virtually no restructuring at all (a miracle in itself). The second marvel is how it intersects with another major landmark of my year 27—the final and only collection of my youthful career as a poet.

I lived in Europe 1975-1980—working, traveling, enjoying myself while going through life's typical and sometimes not so typical ups and downs. I was stationed in West Germany as an enlistee in the U.S. Army, pretty much 9-5 except for duty and alerts, so I could put the uniform aside and travel anywhere on weekends and vacation days. My travels took me to Paris (often), and many other places including Luxembourg, Frankfurt, Brussels, Berlin, Verdun, Speyer, Konstanz, an endless list of the known and less known.

* * * *

I should note that travel was always part of my life. I'd been born in West Germany in 1949, son of a U.S. Army sergeant major stationed in Nurnberg at the time, and an ex-pat mother who was a Luxembourg citizen living in Frankfurt after the war. So I was born a U.S. citizen, but lived my first ten years in various European countries as an army brat. English was my fourth language in life, after Luxemburgish, German, and a smattering of French. My first major pivot at age ten was when my father retired from the Army and we moved to his home city of New Haven, Connecticut. New Haven became my emotional map and experiential lexicon, filled as in anyone's life with both sad and glorious events. In short, New Haven (and more generally New England) were very writable for me. My family left Connecticut in 1972 to retire in the San Diego, California area, and I was to follow in 1974 after a few years spent as a starving artist around New Haven, writing poetry, working as a minimum wage security guard, and pursuing the female of the species (in equal measures probably). I should add the fourth thing, which is that I spent many an evening rambling around student and local bars around the city, drinking cheap beer and laughing raucously with certain cherished drinking pals. By 1973, as I say, I sat in the gas house typing my poetry collection, because I had a sense that I must do this or else they would be forever lost. I probably sensed that, in December 1974, I would pack all of my possessions (including the book of poetry, and a box of unpublished novels) into my old Pontiac and make an epic cross-country trip amid several howling blizzards to San Diego. I did not tarry there long (writing more stuff all the while) but enlisted in the U.S. Army. I was simply not ready to settle down, and I wanted to see Europe again after an epochal absence, and that was the easiest way to accomplish the trip.

* * * *

That is how I ended up in Europe 1975-1980. Forty years ago as of this date—February 2016, which itself will be ancient history soon enough; time to get this show on the road, better late than never—I was a young U.S. enlisted soldier stationed in West Germany. I had the good fortune to miss the tragedy of Vietnam, which ended two days after I enlisted, and to be stationed at a relatively cushy office job in Kaiserslautern. My war was the Cold War, whose realities were with us every day, but underscored to me on a tour of Berlin in 1976.

I served two enlistments there. All of the material here concerns my first enlistment, which was in retrospect the assignment of a lifetime, a dream, to be stationed in Europe, working 9-5 M-F except the usual Army rigmarole, but otherwise free at a moment's notice to drop everything and spend a weekend in Paris, Brussels, Luxembourg, Berlin, Frankfurt, or a thousand other interesting places.

At the same time, I spent many an evening and many hours continuing my life's writing career. By age 27, I already had a poetry writing career behind me or virtually over by then. In 1980, I selected my favorites from among all those poems, and self-published the selection as Pauses: 64 Poems (Copyright © 1980 by John T. Cullen, All Rights Reserved). The publisher (yours truly) was Fresh Press, Kaiserslautern and San Diego. I visited a German printer at the time, bought some supplies, and on his instructions created a primitive case-bound set of no more than a dozen copies, of which I still have a few on hand.

At the same age (27) when I stopped writing poetry, I wrote this glorious, ecstatic, symphonic love story whose manuscript title remained simply Jon + Merile for forty years until 2016, when I am now finally publishing it.

The novel—now titled *On Saint Ronan Street*—was a nostalgic, almost deliriously sad, gloriously emotional and sensual romp into a past that was simultaneously real and imagined, truth and mythological, autobiographical and fictional.

The hero is a young (23) college graduate named Jon Harney with a phantom-limb English degree, limitless energy, a minimum wage job, and an idealistic passion to become a famous poet. He falls into a hopeless but lyrical and wonderful love affair with a beautiful young married woman named Merile. Her husband is a professor of archeology at Yale University, but is always absent without emotional leave. At the moment, Bill (her husband) is on a dig in remote Australia, and digging all sorts of extramarital chicks in Sydney. In fact, he calls her to say he wants a divorce, before he calls her to say he doesn't. Merile is understandably alone, up in the air, and just in time for a wild, crazy, breathless tumble with the Poet. You get the connection.

Here's my flash of insight, which completed the connection between novel and selection.

I was finishing the edits on *On Saint Ronan Street* just this week (late February 2016; update 1 May 2016) and it occurred to me that throughout the novel, I have Jon Harney (under his pseudonym as the alleged Russian émigré poet Charles Egeny) claiming that he is a passionate and aspiring poet, but how do I show that?

I realized that I should sprinkle a small selection of Jean-Thomas Cullen's poems (from Cymbalist Poems) into the text of the novel. I promised to tell you the special, wonderful insight that made the intersection work and the connection click. That's it—I put some real poems into the novel, and I am telling you about the novel here in my larger poetry collection. One day, I will probably make available some more of those old poems from a lost age.

What this does for me is amazing, in my view. It rescues my poems from ignominious (agnominious?) obscurity. At the same time, it adds tremendous juice to the batteries of one Charles Egeny, a.k.a. Jon Harney, a.k.a. yours truly (mythologically sort of). Call it validation. In this grandiose stroke, I was thus able to complete the circuit and close the connection between my to "27" books.

At my website www.27duet.com, I will add more information for lack of room in this brief preface. The title *27duet* is of the book containing both the novel and poems under one cover—also available soon in print and e-book editions.

INTRODUCTION 2014

The poet spent a chaotic post-World War 2 childhood in Luxembourg and other European countries as the son of a U.S. Army service member and a European mother. His mindset was devoutly ritualistic (Catholic), yet blissfully free-thinking, at least as early as age eight. Of those incense-wreathed and stained glass hours only a fragment of earliest poetry survives. Ironically, the city is only about 75 miles from Arthur Rimbaud's childhood drama in Charleville-Mézières, Ardennes, France.

As an adolescent in Connecticut, Jean-Thomas Cullen (a.k.a. John T. Cullen) attended the R.C. high school of Notre Dame, West Haven—but wrote in a secular style that preserved the pieties and fervor of the earlier while painting freely the world as it presented itself.

The high period came during a fragmented post-Beat college presence (or absence in all but body). Alternately haunting coffee shops and book stores, when not hitchhiking among the concrete pillars and cold lights of a clockless time, he wrote of women and discoveries, empires and memories real or imagined. He belonged to no school except the jazz itself that pattered strongly in his mind and blood. The poems speak for themselves—that is why they are poems.

One week in his early 20s, while working as a security guard at an industrial cathedral in New Haven Harbor, he brought in a typewriter and a cardboard box full of scribblings, and—amid the industrial steam and savagery of this old haven—committed hundreds of penned or penciled scraps (napkins, cards, school paper) to a typed journal in between clock rounds where hummocks of dirty ice lay over frozen gravel. He carried this bound thesis with him on a solitary drive to California, and then on a flight over gilded, rosy clouds to Europe.

Five years later, in his late 20s, he wrote the last few poems while stationed far off in West Germany during the Cold War. He had written several novels by then, and folded his entire sheet of music into the prose that occasioned his hours by a cold gray barracks window, listening to Mozart in the autumn river of his blood.

At that time, he selected what he felt were the best of his best, and published them in a small, hand-bound volume titled Pauses. A third of a century (over half a lifetime) later, he made a similar pass through, and selected the same poems again—he had been right in 1980 about his choices. From undine memory, he even corrected a few adolescent syllables to move back to precisely where they had originally been written, so that was right too.

See also: *Notes*, at rear.

LUXEMBOURG
(c1956)

Making faces.

1.   WIR EHREN DICH

(fragment)

Iesus, wir ehren dich

Fur jeden Lanzenstich.

Mit deinem Blut und deinen Schmertzen

Hast du reingewaschen unsere Herzen…

Age 7, Luxembourg

WEST HAVEN

(1960s)

2.   SATURDAY FEAST IN LITTLE POLAND

I watch each Saturday in Little Poland
at Allen's Peerless Junk.

It's a ghoulish feast (before lunch)
of licking, lapping flames,
small bodies in the open pit.

They crouch upon a vast
glittering fallen Goliath with
his armor and his baubles -

(You can almost see the giant limbs outstretched,
   a hand upon a sodden chest,
   and think of that
   sausage jumping
   in the bubbling pan at home) -

Chewing little rubber, paper, oilcloth islands
and cardboard cliffs
with rippling, snapping jaws,
but seeming to devour little.

Jean-Thomas Cullen

Black, smelly smoke whirls upward,
hot within a cold aseptic wind

Etching in summer
inky filth on a humid sky;

In autumn,
dark warmth in cold gray air;

In winter
disappearing into streams of falling snow
that cover the lukewarm scrap heap with
a grayish film;

In spring
Green:
testimony to the new by old things burning.

That's all year round at Allen's Peerless Junk
on Pilsudski Street
near the black old iron railway bridge.

So come, won't you,
come with me, our bellies empty,
and we'll watch the flames this Saturday
(thinking of bubbling kielbasa)
feasting before their week-long fast.

ND 1964/65

3. ALIEN

Velvet currents, silver bubbles
   in the deep
   below an amber water sky...
!To stand on a pearl dust planet
A million miles below a certain
              bobbing bow...
Alone
Among a billion fleeting shapes,
   Alien,-
   (darting silver daggers
     gaping rusty discs
     hacksaw wings...)
   Here is death a quiet dream
   (barracuda fins
     puffs of red dark
     devil teeth gleaming through)
   the end of nothing.
Alien, I!
among the shards of Eden!

ND 1964/5?

                    Jean-Thomas Cullen

4. AUTUMN RIVER

Swirling roundly, river flow,
by cobbled banks
and marshy shores,
racing like the clouds
in the cold grey wind;

    Standing windblown in the eddies
    at your swollen rim,
    reeds and swamp grass lean,
    beaten by the spray of
    foam boats rolling by;

Running moody, River talk
to fish laid on the banks, and
wild geese darting in the gray...
Under wharves and bridges, 'round
small boats backing as
you roll along;

Gripping frothy waves with
curling fingers ride
dying leaves, drifting
from the marsh stream in a circle
then into your center stream;

Dark waters, run along,
with your booty on your heaving back,
squawking as you rumble, but faintly
for the noise you make:

Festive turkeys stolen from the farm,
bucking boxes from the pier, and
trees you've bitten off with
grinding teeth of thunder;

Happy am I, with
my net ashore, and
my dinghy on the wharf, and
my pantry filled for winter feasts:

Godspeed, Autumn River!

1965/6 ND

Jean-Thomas Cullen

5. INTERPLAY

Green expanse,
  shimmering glass
    roof.

Wind there is,
  water runs
    nowhere.

Glimpses:
  Cherub face
    vanished in water;

Age-green watery metal fixtures:
Victorian cherub, youth,
green with age, what is this vision?

Trees, over the flat roofs away,
green and young beyond wetness
  in wind.

Cherubs: trumpeting memories,
Nautilus shells filled
  with tomb ash   and yet

    green leaves
    scrubbed and dripping
    in cleansing wind!


```
                    ND 1966? Rooftop/study hall 3fl
                    over gym *or* some Yale college?
```

6.　　LUXEMBOURG

On a table standing in the grass —
Victorian bones of wood clashing with
　　　　spider blades -
Rests the sky rocking softly
　　as the ever lightly haze
　　brought forth from tremors of vastness
　　echoes from an empty hall filled with
　　silent wind
　　　and colors.

Wind
behind my eyes
fills my forehead with hair
waxes my cheeks
dries my lips

From the village where the people live
the church bell is ringing noon:

Wafting sensations of stew, of sauce, of
meat, unstoppered wine, sense of
　being somewhere else or nowhere
(hunger) but how possibly in this place?

The hay, the hay, Jean Pierre
The tails off the carrots, quick!
Come, children, we shall pray;
Eat, for it is given;
yes, the fields

ND66/67?

　　　　　Jean-Thomas Cullen

7.   SAND AND SUN

When
a dog ambles across
scathing sand with wagging tail
head bowed before the booming breakers
turning clumsily on four legs to
catch the brilliant sun, full on
a friendly canine face
pale tongue

when old weary legs lie stretched from
a wall worn by sand and wind
feet encased in old black lace-ups
feet tired
and sun makes tired and wine makes tired
and eyes make tired

Sleep

Sleep - grit has lost its teeth
wind is like warm water -
warm
tingling mixture
barking happily

ND67ish?

8. ANCIENT POETS

What do the cracked poetries,
the broken rumblings and mumblings
fleshy buttered lips of Catullus,
windy time streets of Ovidean evenstill,
  tell ME,
who gaze at the crescent moon
dipping its scimitar sail
on the wind-blue sea
of the beautiful city
     city of towers
     city of showers
     brief and sun-flecked,
     city of white ramps and bone arches
     whose immensity spells breathless?

Jean-Thomas Cullen

(Catullus —
 your sparrow never looks up,
 hassling breadcrumbs
 earned sweat-drenched on the latifundia,
 in the microcosm courtyard;
 in these walls
 grasses indefinite as Gallic rain:
 Here is every blade, indeed, a blade of grass.)

(Ovid —
 I dream of
 golden apples
 & fleeting white limbs   tinged with
 borrowed shades of light)

Still, the alleys are blue bone,
though you are
both so many centuries still now, quiet,
I only wish I could ask you questions
about life and love.

NHJC summer 1967/8?

STORRS

(1968-1972)[1]

---

[1] University of Connecticut, Storrs

9.   SEES ITSELF

conch of consciousness:
two-edged *
　flitting sea-scissor,
　sword of existence *
　in the dread shallows:

That * instant
(round the wall)
retreat *

And sees itself.

?Storrs 1967/8?

Jean-Thomas Cullen

10. OFFICE MUSIC

&
60¢
steno success

open
spring door
Coca Cola
/
skirt
hi,
**(see p.

dominant and.
stocks bru bra
broke the
!
typo'
bond paper
desk calendar

"Coffee with)

open door
Spring
voices
"While I

a fly!
want to close
the door please?

Musics #3/Spr68/Davenport

11. COMPOSITION I

on a white wall:
switches, three:

OFF, ON, ON

Musics #10/Spr68/Davenport

Jean-Thomas Cullen

12.   WEST HAVEN

there was some minor civilization already
when still only oystermen dredged the green Sound:

tucked-away deep and warmer breeding places;
sea-weathered piers; small gray houses;
where desperate shrubs in dark green armor
eat the aggregate cliffs, and in the tidal marsh:

cold wind picks his way between tall reeds,
turtles crawl, salt water grinds
    half-finished arrow-heads

coons prowl, owls howl, Winter dots the beach
with ice puddings, Spring pebbles the sand
with snails commuting on the tides,
Summer: Oil, sharks, jelly fish, and the
mating ritual of August king crabs by night,
Autumn: driftwood

and on Ocean Avenue, under the trees,
    chestnuts,
    ankle tide of sifting leaves,
over the pavement wind by day, moon by night,
pumpkins, overturned boats, dark football
imitations of war

                                                    1970?

13.   YOUR EYES (ENNUI)

Your eyes are not on fire;
you sit with lyre in lap
leaning against the window

where evening's sun nectars
deepen, making you drunker;

My eyes chance to caress
your white thighs, soft breast,

your belly all tawny
and honeyed in that opiate light.

Your-eyes are lustrous,
half-closed;
No there is nothing to exchange
more reddish than glances;

And so will you remain,
lazy and reclining between
amber curtains, panes of glass.

1970?

Jean-Thomas Cullen

14. HOT DOG VENDOR ON THE BEACH

The wealth was in the hot dog vendor's hands:

Timmie   had big round blue eyes

      bought two   ate his

    gave one to little Janie who

    broke hers

      gave part to   ate hers

     Spotty the dog-

    and so there were three.

McM?1970

15.   JAZZ TRUMPETER

Jazz Trumpeter at climax of a
particularly demanding solo:

<u>Heow!</u>

(lips to the horn,

puts his lips to the horn)

<u>Heow!</u>

Camus 1970 Spring

Jean-Thomas Cullen

16.   THE WISH

As it always will,
summer rain reminds
of autumn thoughtfulness.

Sudden chill, darkness,
uneasy wind in the leaves,
the unease mere melodrama…

because all is and was as
it was and always will be -
Man, and the Wish to Be.

Unk Storrs 1970ish

17.   REDISCOVERIES

That
which discovered long ago
smells good, again and again

That which rediscovered
after once found
long ago and with
ooh and aahh
never loses
its power to surprise
again and again

What was once given
is given again
and again,
coming in disguises
or at a different hour,
on a different train maybe,

but this fresh
ever market
again and again,
Morning,
or Spring sunshine
or a new Love,

it feels so good again,
and never lose the
pebble to enchant!

?Storrs 1970ish?

Jean-Thomas Cullen

18.   SUN WORSHIP/empire

We worship the Sun.
Even in our architectural criminalities
   is justice, as in the dagger's shining eye.

All light is the light of atoms and stars.

The moon and the knife
share splendor's distance.
The knife is on the Earth's dark side
— stabs but she does not whimper —
and the knife is
   miles, miles from the Sun,
   miles from the Moon.

The Moon is an eerie dream of the Earth head.
The knife is carried by a lunatic messenger,
   who built the pyramids,
      drowsing tortoise herd in the desert.
      In the Sun.

But the Sun also shines
on the archaic sky line of New York.

   The winds there
(the windows are opera glasses)
   sing songs of empire.

McM70Spr

Welcome, World, with all your vinegar!
Welcome, Reality, triumphant beast!
Welcome, Sunlight, feast of splendor!

After the deep galaxies of my brainself
are done exploding
And the abrupt, calamitous young stars
    finished with their wild music

Welcome, subtle golden sunlight
who sting my narrowed eyes,
and ride the sweet summer wind in the
leaves, green airport of insects!

There is, after all, only one fate,
one destiny, bereft of gods and devils,
free of angels, demons, deaf to prayers,
mysterious to squinting diviners.

Jean-Thomas Cullen

This is my destiny, limited but honored credit,
to take upon my shoulders if I chose —
    and choose I do,
like Bunyan wrapping the ox around his neck.
I want to carry my fate beyond the fence
toward the looming green-black forest
beyond the symphony of my best years.

As the dull black cipher
unfolds into a mighty dream,
so there is, again and again, only morning
to drive the night away: Precise,
rich in changing colors,
vibrant and harmonious guitar,
the well-tuned life.

All things, from here, follow of themselves:
Dawn the night which follows day,
insight the dull cipher,
perfect mnemosyne the splendid here and now!

Storrs?1970ish?

20. THE WORLD NOT RIGHT

The world was never right,
I guess

In the good old days
the devil was loose
roaming the world
seeking the ruin of souls

one awoke at night
sweating in dread
at the howl of a dog
chained to a fence
at the edge of town
edge of the world

where men have set foot
on the moon
was an alien planet
thought to be a face
made of cheese,
with unknown terrors, tygers,
behind fitful running clouds,

Jean-Thomas Cullen

where today
against the sweet silver moon
runs a gleaming 707
easily surmounting
the dark turquoise sky

We who huddled in caves, cold,
afraid even of warming fire
poured from the sky by our
generous sky father/earth mother,

afraid we were, afraid we are,
still all the old instincts,
still that sweating in the night,
world not right, never right,
poor world, poor us.

Storrs 1970ish

21.   NEW HAVEN

East Rock: Cannon eyes overlooking the city
with its sea; its forests and rivers.

Indian Head: Old gun emplacements,
   where a stick to the hillside
   will turn the loam, expose bones and
   arrow heads damp with seasons;

Old stone bridge & winding 1890 promenade
& rock slides & abandoned road.

::::600 years after Leif: Wood ships on the
Connecticut River, landing at the red light
near College Street and Frontage Road;
settlement; prayer; wharves, warehouses;

::::in the 1600s a ghost ship was seen foundering
in a stormy night. Fires were lit on the rocks
and boats set into the brine bristling with
boat hooks but ship and storm and night passed,
by day men returned sculling under sour clouds.
Days later the ghost ship
upside down and under full sail   crossed in a
rainbow several times by Morris Cove.

Jean-Thomas Cullen

::::Turn of the century: Morocco; Long Wharf;
Smedley's warehouse; where horses shipt raw
from the West were broken by Nutmeg cowboys.

::::Connecticut River changed course. The ancient
bed is now Exit One, Downtown, where Hooker knelt
End pray'd, wellspring of I-91, super highway,
whose glass/metal waves roll into foggy Vermont.

Today
on the overpass,
smog fishes   with beak
   and lays new eggs.

1970

22.   LAVENDER EXPRESS

Lavender express, hear me in your dignity:
I abuse time, am buffeted (and your shoulder
   is hard as the next) but none my fault.

Take then my bitter tendrils, my roots, shoots,
my herbal corona, unbury me from the wires;
I have stopped, and am ready to start over.

1970?

Jean-Thomas Cullen

23.   PEAR PICKING SEASON

(fragment)

at random, a luxury:

hands in the fence, shaking
clustered leaves, gnarly twigs

as glistening sticky
globes dangle

then drop
plop plop
one by one.

Coventry Fall 1970

24.   FOR COMPANIE

Fingers smelling of wood swarths,
like bacon from the fireplace,
She kept me Companie;

In the room in the cottage,
in that roome by the lake,
she kept me Companie;

Round-breasted, rumpled white sweater
  stuck with bits of autumn leaf,
  alive with borrowed fire colors*

  (* and we catalog the burning of
    fires, and homeliest
    is wood burning in fire places,
    food in iron places,
    bacon and chestnuts, wood
    and auburn hair, such a girl was she)

Her hair, her sweater, warm, emanent
with fragrance of fresh leaf
and common burning wood: Wine
from Madeira, Virginian tabacos,
were shipt to us,
for Companie!

Coventry winter70

25.   COLDFALL

I see
whirling autumn leaves
a turning clock

I see
turning autumn leaves
a whirling clock

Night has fallen
the cold is come

a batting of the
eyes —
not more

a pointing finger in
a window vibrating with frost:
Night is come
the cold has fallen

Nibbling nights with fresh-bread breath
fumbling figures standing in snow
darkness has come
darkness has fallen

the cold

?Storrs or NH 1970ish?w?

26. SPRING FEVER

(fragment)

Softly visits the gurgle-bird,

spring gently presses,

heartbeats quicken in

the quilted hay-yield,

Spring gently presses.

Camus 2.19.71

Jean-Thomas Cullen

27.   RACE

I became conscious of your race
            briefly
confronted by your spread thighs
your sun-yellow curls.

I am dark-haired,
descendant of Kelts and Saxons;
    You
    of Angles~ Farthest Thule.

When I saw your moon-white curls
thought of your fairness soured
    (briefly, precious vessel)

I remembered your snow-haired warriors
whom my people fought.

71?Camus

28.   COURTLY LOVE

The words are spoken from our fingertips:

Love, you are best to be with.

You are swift in piercing, hunter —

my heart seeks you everywhere.

Pictures, portraits,

lutes, and pergaments;

White stag bleeding on the rocks;

Two lances broken in his side.

Spring1971

Jean-Thomas Cullen

29.   SHIPPER

   stately sailing captain of the line,
he sh'd'f s'd he borrowed night from night,
blacker breath than icy coal barge,
and flecked, by star, wif beer spots.

Turns he, Dane/bearded and sez:
"Harum," - this by way of pipe tar sediment -
"Alter's outen Afta by bright bell Scorpion."

:::sell me no stick to stir yr mire, ape, I,
I travel on the wave tables,
I log the ice floes under Comae.

Ferial night - shiver; boreal; aureal;
crawl, whight, to your tree and see
what siren combs stir my so pocketable waves.

Storrs/Camus? Fall/Winter 71/72?

30.   NOCTURNE

Your wind, my empty friend,
come to fill my open hands—
the night is his bellyful purse,
come to clatter pennies on my knuckles.

The mountains in the city have neon.

A trumpet is still, I know, because
because of his hand, to her breast,
and her hand, rising to caress.

An empty coat's the wind's tent,
air in trumpet's wet with osculations,
he signed his name and
folded the canvas away.

Somewhere, I think, butterflies
    and children.

Gomez saw and heard the elevation.
Eddie cried and sang and drank
    into his radio.
I am a stranger here
but these streets treat me
as if I'd never been away.

8/9/71 3 a.m.

Jean-Thomas Cullen

31. INDIAN SUMMER

Summer is Indian).
the weather is mild

September is the last
Indian, I guess

Like any of us

Mild,

and Conquered.

Coventry, 1971, Fall

32.   COLLEGE YOUTH AGO

That gone ecstasy, that madness under the

    hill's lip.

Homer's ships tried these shores in vain.

Sails furled, silence made them

    drift away.

The beer cans sank before dawn.

Pink dawn: Dinosaur buildings

    frozen in mist.

1971?

Jean-Thomas Cullen

33. FLIGHT LINE

In this tangled life maybe,
one touch of beauty,
or a hint of the Great Love,
for the much so indistinct,
the sky, this is surely planet love;

I want to hook
    into you
    my sky line
and give you gas
so you turn gold and groan:
Hey_____

Which is, after all,
the reward,
the hook-up, the sky flight,
my love to yours, you
who I am not.

1971?

NEW HAVEN

(1971-1975)

34 . NIGHT CITY CLARION

— ?where were you, she, warm, says.
— !I was, I say, crawling in the girders,
  the night city.

Head open, friendly February,
Mild flavors of Spring night, intimations
cleaned of nicotine & able to savor the

  (cocktail music used to clean blue ring
  bouillon dish
  in burnt-ash dust-carpet old doorman
  hotel-) air.

February, febris, feverary, early fever,
And all that old ragtime face,
leaning out with the shredded wall ads,
from the doorway,

The Town, Old, covered always with yesterdays
and yesterday's words, her ads,
  her thought balloons.

  Mannequins, my ballet,
  downtown , the empty streets,
  friendly lovers promenade, steak
  and violins, old wine, cellophane,
  wrap the windy streets in fog sheets.

Foggy night, cat steps,
eyes in the fishbowl, rondeau,
MY MIND IS SO PAST IDEOLOGY!

In fog, invasion fleet: cadillacs,
  minesweeper gowns, gents with

Jean-Thomas Cullen

                    carnation semaphore,
               To the opera! And where, really, succeed?

  (I just don't know,
  not too strongly, I,
  I just don't know,
  not strongly at all.

Sky rain: Tinkle as it falls,
early warning: pull in the newspapers,
the News is pulled to safety,
only strong as the paper it's printed on.

Alto sax.
Tiffany bubbles.
Tap room—closed.

No new mythologies
—disbelief is sleep—
old-myths-sag-in-fog.

Cadillacs, for the Easter visit, early:
In the fond night, dreams of spring.
Innocents, we, phantoms of the old new faith,
nets we are to gather airy alphabets.

Alone, along the fog streets,
tripping only on ultimate acids
of the body trip;

Roll out the Puto,
and Haul up the Sum!

Not heartless at all, but no longer feeling
cold, nor darkness, nor the city, or people,
nor messages, nor saxophones.

In the city,
In the city,
In the night city,
and. phantoms in every chrome elbow.

Flowers, Flowers for the city —
bring Brussels, Paris, Berlin,
Rome, Vienna, and London:
all the dreams, memories, the museum,
stacked here, the curator is
blundering old Jonny Tundaboid,
75¢ expert whose fingers and lips
probe cracked sidewalks
looking for, not his, nor Clark Kent's,
but old Dream King's footprints.

I circle, oblivious of history,
waiting for Spring (papers in the rain)
wheels out on the blind air,
waiting for the landing light.

Waiting for the words to dissolve
like salt on my cheeks, the rain.

Open, City:
Open, receive the rain:

Your flowers,
last blown kisses,
as you sail from your harbor.

Feb71New Haven?

Jean-Thomas Cullen

35.   SAMBA OF SHADE

agua e umbras - this I drink, from your shade,
oak trees, the very sun is chlorophyl green,
the wind is warm, moist, wrapping itself
like the juice of ripe, thick leaves
around my hungry pores.

   The mysterious bird's throat
is the secret Eleusynian well
and a mirror to   quaint water gurgles.

   In a turban of opiate heat
I release my swollen head to alight in tall reeds.

There, black mud weighs
   The black mud among my footsteps
weighs my impositions on Maat's scale
            balanced by tall reeds.

   The self, the will, are in the clouds,
harmless, evanescent, my thoughts like bees.

   Evenings are wind-drawn
in the mature organic processes of my thoughts.

Swallows, arriving north for Spring,
have, in truth, no mind for precedent.

Spring72Schiavone's

36.   CHRISTMAS

That fresh drizzly foggy night
it was Mona and me
and Henry brought the tree.

Mona and me
(we are ever innocent
of our so many tomorrows)
and Henry heisted a tree.

To the warm house
we brought the tree.
It was too big and
I drove with the top down.

To get it through the door
we had to cut it in half.

There was just too much,
everything too much,
in that little place, good nook,
we drank our beer and passed
the hours, Mona and me,

Later making love
   (after Henry went home alone)
under the tree.

NH 1971Xmas

Jean-Thomas Cullen

37. LOST LOVE

(icy moment)
Ruthlessness has no cuttinger edge

than a love reconspired alone

and cut from itself

in the ice

Of rediscovered solitude.

Schiavone's Spring 72 PostBP

The dull oak by its trembling leaves
dreams the acorns' bounding gonadity.

Drunk on sunlight, we climb the mast.
We scan, tattered, for passing virgins.
The horizon, however, has shrunk;
all is but a dream, a prayer,
the reenactment is a resignation.

A strong, narrow-eyed youth climbed the oak.
He saw the ship and sailed.
Later as a young man he fell captive to love
   in a Berber queendom. A vengeant king
soon came and slew the youth.

Ever after, a quiet man with troubled eyes
   paces the island's tropic rim.
   With binoculars he scans the mainland.

The youth's grave is but
   a shallow plot of turned earth
   and the leaves shake, rattling, over it,
   the man visits it often.

The king's spear lies gross and green
in the ocean rim.

Sea horses dance in the boiling waters,
   conches sleep on the deep highways;
No virgin waves in the misty distance.

3-20-73 G&H

Jean-Thomas Cullen

Men recently emerged from the sea
tend to sunshine, vanilla, and soft company

Men who have swum ashore
like to head home in late afternoon
carrying striped bags, ice cream cones.

Men
leaving their armor, their halberds,
pitards in steaming salty sand,
like to dry themselves before the screen doors
of shops dry and scoured inside
   like the gleaming chestnut she11
   redolent chic cork, leather, polished driftwood.

But come time, they back against the sea,
arms spread to the stone cliffs.

Silently, reluctantly, they take their armor
    from the sand,
    wrap themselves in drying cords
    and belts
    of moss-green sea weed,
    pick up their king crab shells and
    barnacle-and-scallop crusted tridents,
      and walk slowly
      into the deepening tide.

When cars are parked and naked knees cooling
           under kitchen tables,
    The sun drifts to rest
    among tangled trees.

A buoy abandoned on a sand bar
comes to life with the tide.

The waves of the sea are briefly bowls to the sky.

The closing of the waves
Over the last wave of a limp hand
is the merciful end to a lingering goodbye.

Spr72/postBP

              Jean-Thomas Cullen

40. PIANO

My thoughts played piano
long and softly from your eyes.
I could have put your apples in a jar
but there were places to stay
(while you chafed to go)
and you left
(you said you would)
me in poetic triumph

1971or2?

41. LOST LOVE

(timeless moment)

The hearth is visible.

You, fine girl, broke the flowers

which became running greyhounds

at the wetted fireplace.

```
?72NH/postBP?
```

Jean-Thomas Cullen

42. SINGLES BAR

Are you going early, and alone?

<u>Stay</u>. We
  are the driftwood of
  conversation, fragments of
  ambitions, broken halves,
  the late lamp. In this
  our deep and distant eyes
  glanced to agree.

<u>Stay</u>. My voice
  is inaudible, but my eyes
Are screaming.

G&H late 72

43. DOGGING HER

…Dogging her: we are all Indians.

Early cold whispering into wood confessionals
respells morbid and groping presexuality.

Far cities (cold nights,
stale beer, intimation French fries,
gurgling wharf walks) fresh air:
New Haven, New Haven, Port Nouveau,
reenactment, resignation:

    All potential resolved
    combination by combination
    by pairing, intersection, erasure,
    short circuit, to the one final
    bumper stop. Stop.

Jean-Thomas Cullen

Realizing mortality is the first true gesture,
the last spontaneous action: We are dogs
ambling in alleys of time
Caught in the autumn and evening
before spring and day are satisfied.

…Dogging her:
O thee, O thou, we dog her heels,
and she is mortal (dagger, oh truth!)
if and only if
to the autumn mind,
rusty leaf, snow flake, compass,
crucifix, structure and coembodied purpose,
rimed ice, black iron hinges,
cage
of minutes, days, and hours.

Oh and she has blonde hair-fall,
milk skin stippled pink by cold's seduction,
blue and guiltless eyes.

Her body is perfect,
statuary,
we dog her heels,
she too is only human,
we devour her shattered condescension.

?New Haven/72ish

44.   CAFE MACHO

Man of great deeds, o violent life!
He sees his story as one of drink and smoke:
precipitous, with red nights and lightning days;
painful encounters with careless or impulsive women;
friends with guns - he is of battlements,
    sailing ships, and cannonades!

Women (when they see him lingering
            with his Marlboro
            over an expensive drink)
think: there
sits a gentle and unsuccessful man.

New Haven 1972ish

Jean-Thomas Cullen

45.   CAFE MACHO

Your string has fallen,
pharaonic dancing girl,
I see your tan skin
in the flute music;

in the liquor,
the dusky lounge,
the airconditioned dance place
with women to pick from,
pastiche of loves
that might have been
were it not for…

What tender celebration
if you were you
and I were I
but here we are all
the should be,
the would be, and may be…

She walks out to accept this dance,
her eyes are black and fierce,
her beauty is terrible, ringing,
like an army with banners flying.

She deigns to accept this embrace
from the ninety-ninth shadow
of the man she gave her soul.

O essential grace,
the jazz of your dry skin
is beige and angled in motions.

You evoke, essential grace,
music; it was I, once,
who took your soul.

For the space of a dance,
the embrace of a trance,
quite by chance,
we relive my long ago night
and some evening of yours

before you had your hair cut and styled,
when you possessed your youngest beauty.

Your smile is a white feather
floating in my air-conditioned eyeballs.

Your tan and tennis face
is full of invitations,
reasons, address cards.

?New Haven 1972ish

Jean-Thomas Cullen

46.   REFRIGERATOR

Paired Towers of Health:
   a quart of orange juice
   a quart of milk -
   beaded with cold droplets -
On a hot summer afternoon.

Unk?NH1972ish/reflOrangeSt1962ish

47. BIRTHDAY

(fragment)

I begin to feel
measureless loss of youth -
itself
abdication from jeweled childhood.

NH Canner Street 1972 Fall

48. NEW HAVEN HARBOR

Your death, broken horse, on the iron tracks,

defines the meaning of the Sun;

The nature of your blood, the Moon.

Your torn brown hide, leather already,

says that something happened

      which is now past.

Something is now past.

?NH Harbor 1973?

49.   MOVING IN

This is a stark place.
The room is empty and the night cold,
   autumn chill smells of leaves,
   the only light is that of the moon
on a hard polished wooden floor.

the music is a vagary of tentative
piano notes from some other existence,
some other apartment of
neighbors not yet known.

Sing to me softly, radio,
devoted presence which
hull us both against the cold.

Jean-Thomas Cullen

This is a stark place,
a new place, an inbetween place.
Much is left behind but of
the new world there is nothing yet,
only gleaming promise on
moonlit wooden floor, .
hinted smells of wax and paint
    and autumn leaves,
    unaffected piano notes
    unaware of my intruding ear.

Sing to me, softly,
envelop me, hull us,
for this moving,
dread moving, the nothing new
and nothing old, the autumn cold,
all things had to be left behind,
and this is a stark place.

                    ?Piano Music prob MrsBurgey's Hamden73/4

50.   EVERSCENES: The Silver Surfer

Memorex MacOedipus, to an Older Woman
(while sating on music, beer, snow,
          and pork shoulder)

Self calls, future,
free myself: your
cloying musky fingernail love,
cruel and malignant unselfsufficiency,
big scared wet black eyes,
panic reaction, cage of frenzy,
parsimony of time,
salty electrolysis my own crumbling teeth…

Wham, Bam, Thank you Ma'am,
durling, yes, I AM the Silver Surfer,
shoot between the stars,
a hairless gleaming oscar;

Jean-Thomas Cullen

I am the award, the reward,
rider on the silver board,
shoot between the stars,
pound your unpopulated beach,
rock against your trampoline;
your reaching eyes,
your encaverned thoughts seek my
          flying form.

Yearning
from the head of your Albert and Victoria
steams around my silver torso.

     I am in the transporter room,
younger than you, my bald silver head
glows in your round animal eyes — my, baby,
streamlined godlike face.

I could be lost in you,
silver needle, jet, arrow plane in
               your late sun,
Daedalus I am you melt my wings,
yours are thunder and lightning.

I am dawn, man, immortal, and you
   the dying dusk.
I will not lie in your arms, die by
   your charms;
you move me, you BEHOOVE me,
Ulysses dazed and oil-drenched in
    Circe's bed, wed,
but I, yes, AM the Silver Surfer,
sky master, cloud skipper,
I surf above your bleeding earth
touched by the welcoming warmth
   rasped by tigress claws…

A dozen arrows pierce my shining legs,
   my beautiful legs;
as I fly away silvery, hard, youthful
   and without mercy,
I am stained with the lingering golden
    afterglow
of your broken heart.

New Haven 1974

KAISERSLAUTERN

(1975-1980)

51.   ELAN

Afra-Shemuth: The cat made syllables
  pouting its undulating hackles
  by the mahogany chair leg.

The rug, where she practiced her claws,
  burnt if you ran a finger over it.

  Coffee was made
and betrayed
my need to escape.

  Tobacco was made to glow,
shimmering blue smoke wreaths
in the motionless air: I despaired
          of escape:

          Turned traitor
          to my moment,
          to my hours,
waited, burning in tobacco, didn't want
to meet her parents.   Read old
glossy magazines slick with ad promise:

Jean-Thomas Cullen

Afra-Shemuth: The ad man
bought clay, blue at Stonehenge,
powdered the rich Canadian birches,
smeared Penna charcoal into ink,
bought glossies, Apollo resplendant,
the ad man laid the message
on the mahogany table top, wreathed
  in shimmering blue smoke wreaths:

Afra-Shemuth: The Pomade
of Stutz owners, Harvard Pendant,
on White Field, Gloved Hands at the
Wrist Couped, Letter H, Gules...

Afra-Shemuth: Unkempt but fair?
Afra-Shemuth: Seeks affair?

Don't despair.
Rub it in your hair.
It's the bear grease with flair.

Unk Late/KTown?

52.   SOME LATE HOUR

Loneliness is trumpets. Fire in loins.
Silence is music, the creeping time.
I need to embrace but no one is here.
T know no sweet soul lost in mine,
no arms and eyes warmly reach for me.

I am alone in a foreign land,
in a city others hold dear since childhood.

That I left my own dear city
means my soul is hot and dry, a
fevered thing yearning for water.

Home is far, far, on the day side of the world
and all the unseen whistling jets
are going there tonight.

No one can embrace the moon or the stars;
their warmth is shed elsewhere.

No one can bear the silence or the fire,
the trumpets, the music, heat in belly,
and soul like baking stones.

No one can ask time, no one speaks with
silence, no one can be happy alone.

Ktown 1975ish?

Jean-Thomas Cullen

53. ARMY AND AIR FORCE IN SOUTHERN GERMANY

Autumn leaf sunlight:
here in the forest
where some Roman maniple may have rested,
evening cookery, where the seasons
are as epic yet.

Willowy Cardumnii women walked with water pots
and later the rosy, beaked Germanii.
Here. This well of retrospection,
this eternal mud, foggy winter, bronchitis,
while our pine-imprisoned armor sinks rusting
into the slide and slag of brown hillsides.

Here, Mars, Pallas, your arrows poised,
celebrate your curly-haired rebellion, have done!
Those Druids will speak no more,
The pearl-handled colts are Excalibur, sunk
in stone.

The Sun, red head, swims in the frosty jet streams,
Thunder whispers. On the dew, water droplets.
Boom, an omen, Hymen, o Hymenaie, marriage
of moon and lightning, Bangsalot,
campfire tale, and then Cardumnii slumber,
Keltic sleep.

Sleep, Midnight, sleep, Warrior babies,
golden heads and blue eyes, pink wet lips,
until you wake again, gaunt missiles.

Above the transparent storm,
on blue funnels,
spring larks wheel in spirals.

KTOWN 1975/6

Jean-Thomas Cullen

54.   SPRING SUNLIGHT

(fragment)

Sunlight: You spear of introspection,

dream of love,

You long inhalation

and sigh of time!

UNK

55. PARIS

(cities eternal)
In cities eternal,
bright fires are fed

with moth-like people who come,
and dance, and vanish.

Paris, like Rome like San Francisco,
endless pageant, soya feelings
and paper discoveries, soul sponge,
timeless, immortal, when we
are so achingly mortal.

Go Friend leave the City;
find the individuum
away from these words and smiles;
some rotting home sweet home
on a festering river
where you've known every fishing spot,
every place to go parking,
every corner drugstore,
every season, all your life.

Jean-Thomas Cullen

Go to the place
where you first found love.

That wine
was sweeter.
That memory
is dearer.

There is no love among strangers,
no home among monuments,
no sleep under foreign gables.

Go to the place
where you walked with your eyes closed,
where you can die remembered,
where you can live among old friends,
Home, where you came from,
the Only.

UNK/NHorKTown/Dr.Mormile said c1971ish

56.   HOMAGE TO A NUDE

O Cheek and Smile,

ye buttock moon,

orchestra of fingers,

long legs, and pink belly,

pear breasts with stem nipples,

center fold, still life,

still I think it is the

source of light —

your smile.

```
                              KTown 1975/6
                    Playboy Ctfld on wall
```

57.   MID-POINT FOR ODYSSEUS

Where, steady plumb, beaded eye
is mid-point for Odysseus?

He, guileful Danaean, after leaving Circe
and all the ogres of other-destiny,
asks again: Ye dis, is it shore I see,
Penelope's house, where the
long-tongued suitors pant, and, yea,
   she spins?

Spins — unmindful, straight-eyed,
sure of this truth against all others,
the inherent destiny, the fate itself
Odysseus could not see
for her, for him, she spins the cloth,
her wheel is a machine of sparks and stars.

Is it I, he cries, staggering
   from the wine-dark sea,
   dripping and heavy on the pebbled beach,
I, who thought too much?

Is it I who went too far, only to return,
who come alone and disguised
this late hour, this late day?

Where, steady plumb, beaded eye,
is mid-point for Odysseus?

KTown 1975/6

Heidebron (Meadow Fountain): sweet blue eyes,
yellow hair, Frisian smile, Kiel, where, I imagine,
God's drum pounds on the North Sea
and the seething water foams open
under ice and sun
to emit trumpets of Arctic poetry.
A flame burns in the ice.
Your brief nearness taught me an hour of Mozart.
Sea water, briny and smelling of fish,
is decorously sipped in those parlors.
Ladies wear fur and growl in the streets.
O Hanseatic angel, breath of sagas,
your tartan smeared with candle wax
from the night's dancing —

Slender ship, farewell, back to your North.
Like any pale young queen who worship-
ped wooden pantheons under moss and wood,
you have drunk eagerly the blond wines
our gods give us down here in the south.
Briefly you furled your sail,
touched your flying breast against Paris,
sought in the warm and turbulent southern lands
the same vineyards and monasteries sacked by
  snow-haired warriors long ago
and now, laden with treasure,
you will return to the beer-like sea,
the bear woods, the palinged outposts,
the high German music, Hamburch,
  burhuc.

So long, dear spirit,
kindling message, bright fire,
sky eyes, snow hair, sun smile,
meadow fountain, sweet eagle,
forest partridge, smiling, farewell!

KTown 1975/6

59.   ORIOLE FLIGHT

Your oriole flight is
  apprehended;

You fall, banded,
  land on rooftops,
  tar gums yr feathers.

Inca, Inca, your dreams
  are memory, your journey
  is ended, your wings
Are broken
  (never was
  nor ever will be).

?KTown 1975ish?

Jean-Thomas Cullen

60.   TWILIGHT

As light is slowly extinguished
and deep peaceful sleep settles
are all good children home by the fire?

As the night comes,
ragged field of gnawing stars,
heart-breaking stretches of eternity,
are you a close and loving family?

As the immense earth turns and groans
in the stopless bath of solar music,
are you alive and alone and in touch?

Are you in the parade?
Is there not some glow behind your
dark windows, some warm spirit
nosing about the gray old walls?

Before the cold earth takes you down
again to the worms and their merry friends,
is there maybe a dance you'd like to hear,
a song you'd maybe you and me
and just the smiling vinyl orchestra?

Should we think of homeless children
and John Astor suffering from crepititis
or drag a stupid dog sopping from the rain?

Yes, and light a pipe
or maybe type;
  Sing at the piano, foam a beer,
  steam the windows with good cheer

Before we pull up the white sheet
careful, regretful in the darkness,
and slide into our cold bed?

Yes, and only the music,
sweet smiling-music,
as daily each new Columbus
discovers this fertile harbor!

?KTown 1975/6ish?

61.   TESAMON'S TESTIMONY

Time is testimony from simple Tesamon
who died upon Priam's field.
He gave to his wife as she did to him
the time due one another.

What truly captured him
was her love.

They gave to one another time,
and time alone is what is valuable
in this short life.

Those two, they gave each other
their youth, a treasure none may take back.

When he saw she loved him
He melted inwardly,
treasured her gift, for
   once, she was beautiful,
and he never forgot
   how she offered her young years.

Somehow, no greater sacrifice
was ever made.

KTown 1975/6

62. TESAMON'S MOTHER

Sing, simple Tesamon, the baby you were,
the delight you found in life.

The sun's warm rising dispelled the night
so often, when you cried for milk.

Your mother was rich, and gave breast
offering coos when you cried.

Never forget that kind hand which raised you
and those loving words in the dear kitchen.

Like mother, like sun.

Her rays streamed over you, irradiating you,
and the wealth she gave you made you a man.

The anguish of your death under pointed sword
was only your mother's, not yours.
Life was full, because she loved.

KTown 1975/6

Jean-Thomas Cullen

63. GOD OF THE BUILDINGS AND TREES

Underlying the shapes: geometry and poetry
and the good life is a taut guitar,
its strings measured, then bent
by the roaring ocean of perception

The fight with random agglutination
proceeds and a given flower
should be picked from this rushing car

How easy it must be
to read the truth, the way,
and the life from a book

More exciting to wrestle with angels
and love the Lord still as I love me
when I love you loving me o music
and poem, flashing dance, architecture!

Under the words is the ocean
in the ocean are the fishes and
among the fishes are sharks
and glowing things

Where the birds are is the
wild fresh air without order
unless you know the whole
and then, still, the
pro and causa recede infinitely
because there is only so much time
and hormone excitement to play with
all the different clouds

On a meadow in time
are the graves
I visit them
when my piano is alive, electric,
and the good loves are there, my
flesh and. blood and memory -
do you deny me this, God of the Law,
when you made it so?

Do you take my tears of joy
as a prayer when I have good music,
do you maybe
sing and tap along with me, Lord,
when I have found good rhythm
and love all the whole wide world?

Are you happy when I am happy,
when I sing I would be born again
and again if I could I would if I could
again in your world and
the lumen of your numen
is a blaze in my whole this way?

KTown 1975/6

Jean-Thomas Cullen

64. MOTH

You annoyance,
brief,
because after a moment's anger
I reflect on the justice
    of your presumption,
    the dignity of your proclamation,
as you enter your last wild dance,
dervish,
moments before you die thrashing
in the cauldron of desire
around the light bulb.

KTown PanzerKas 1975/6

Photo: San Diego, about 1985, Jean-Thomas Cullen with Carolyn.

NOTES

The dating of the poems is essentially from the typing, in 1974, in New Haven Harbor. For each poem, as I tried to reconstruct its context, sometimes years later, I inserted my best guess as to when and where I wrote it. In many cases, the info was written on, or decipherable from, the original scraps of paper. In other cases, I added my best recollection during the compilation of either 1974 or 1980. In this final edition of 2013, memory is too faint to register, so I am at the mercy of my younger self nearly half a century ago. That poet was at last as on beat as I am today, if not more so. I am surprised to find an uncanny memory-ear for a precise turn of phrase, the right syllable in the right breath, or just the right punctuation *here*, not *there*.

ND stands for Notre Dame West Haven, my high school. UConn stands for University of Connecticut, Storrs, place of my undergraduate studies in English (with relateds in Classics, History, and German). Homer's ships could have been Homer's blue bicycles (1968 Mr. Babbidge bought 100 for all to use, with destructive results). NHJC stands for *New Haven Journal-Courier*, the extinct morning side to *The New Haven Register*. One poem, I think, on a remarkable late afternoon, overlooking briefly sunny rooftops after a rain, as a luminous blue dusk just as quickly grew. Camus was our existentialist monicker for The Campus Restaurant, a now thankfully extinct greasy spoon filled with rotten food, watery coffee, and shady characters. Coventry and Ashford (Hashford) are two Connecticut towns were I lived off campus from UConn for short times. KTown is G.I.-speak for Kaiserslautern, Germany. Mrs. Burgey was an elderly landlady.

Dr. Mormile was a mentor during my early 20s, father of my dear friend (sadly as of 2010 also late) Jim. He had a PhD from Yale (1930ish?), in Romance and Classical Languages. He served with the U.S. Army C.I.C. during WW2, and then made a career with the CIA in Rome. He retired to his home city of New Haven around 1967, and taught part-time at Quinnipiac (then College). Despite his love of Rome, and intimate knowledge of its topology, he told me one homey Thanksgiving Dinner that one should live in a small home place where people are not transient souls as in great cities (Rome, New York, London, Paris, and the like) but are rooted in time and place. It was a magnanimous but melancholic observation, filled with nuance, that I would ever treasure.

(San Diego, January 2014)

San Diego Author John T. Cullen

John T. Cullen—also Jean-Thomas Cullen and John Argo—is a novelist, journalist, essayist, and science and history writer in San Diego, California. His personal web presence dates to 1996 in Internet pioneering days:

www.johntcullen.com

John T. Cullen is the author of over 30 books, as well as dozens of articles (nonfiction) and short stories (fiction). He has written at least one scholarly paper for peer review, on the ancient Sator Rebus—an enigma for which he has provided the first plausible translation and explanation.

He has lived in various countries across North America and Europe, and is conversant in a number of languages including English, German, and Luxembourgeois. He translated Goethe's Faust (Part I) from German into English in an edition to appear from Clocktower Books by 2017.

Appearing as a Clocktower Books original edition by 2017 is his ground-breaking popular work of ancient history, *A Walk in Ancient Rome* (1st Authorized Print Edition)—a readable, accessible topological tour of ancient Rome in the age of Constantine. It goes far beyond other guides that only hit the highlights, usually in a random and surface manner, which only leaves readers confused and no wiser. This virtual tour guide takes the lay or student reader to all fourteen Augustan districts of the imperial capital, often visiting areas known only to experts, for an in-depth understanding of a lost world that was the template for our own. The author vividly explains the history and religious significance of the monuments, streets, parks, temples, and other sites in a structured, disciplined manner like no other book of its type.

In San Diego, he is the first to plausibly explain one of the region's (and nation's) most intriguing puzzle—the ghost story at the Hotel del Coronado, associated with Kate Morgan; but more importantly from his standpoint, the true crime of 1892 that led to the so-called Beautiful Stranger's dark and violent death amid allegations of foul play and sexual dalliances with men in the highest places.

The owner of the Hotel del Coronado at the time was John Spreckels, one of the nation's wealthiest men. Spreckels was in the White House with President Benjamin Harrison, negotiating the future of the sovereign monarchy of Hawai'i, when a ruthless grifter named Kate Morgan and two accomplices tried to pull off a blackmail ploy that went horribly wrong. The result was a cover-up, and a murky, colorful legend that has intrigued the world for over 120 years. The author has written <u>Dead Move: Kate Morgan and the Haunting Mystery of Coronado</u> (Nonfiction) as a scholarly analysis with over one hundred footnotes and endnotes. He followed this up with <u>Lethal Journey</u>, a noir 1890s period mystery based on his notes and the most gripping elements of the long-standing myth.

John T. Cullen holds a B.A. in English (University of Connecticut, Storrs), a B.B.A. in Computer Information Systems (National University, San Diego), and an M.S. in Business Administration (Boston University). He has a workmanlike appreciation of Latin, and a nodding acquaintance with ancient Greek, for research purposes.

He has been an Internet pioneer—the world's sixth digital publisher (Clocktower Books, 1996+). He was for years author of the acclaimed Sharpwriter.com (in 1999 named by Writer's Digest as one of the top 101 resource websites for authors). He was also, for nearly a decade, publisher and editor of Far Sector SFFH—during its heyday, the world's oldest professional web magazine of science fiction, dark fantasy, and horror.

He is being recognized as the first person to ever decipher the mysterious ancient Sator Square, an enigma that has puzzled historians and archeologists for centuries. As an Active Member of International Thriller Writers, at a recent annual convention in New York City, he was probably the only author present who had ever actually deciphered a mysterious, ancient inscription of great importance, found all over ancient Roman empire—and lived to tell about it.

For more information, visit John T. Cullen's website:

www.johntcullen.com/

New: Progressive Thriller Genre

John T. Cullen in 2016 invented a new form of thriller, the Progressive Thriller, with the launch of a new novel *Valley of Seven Castles, a Luxembourg Thriller* in 2016. Visit the website

www.progressivethriller.com

The Progressive Thriller category teaches us uncomfortable truths about the rapidly disintegrating halo under our corporate-induced imperial hallucinations, like exceptionalism, and other national delusions that make a tiny number of oligarchs wealthier, while reducing the vast majority to novel forms of serfdom in a new world odor reeking suspiciously of medieval feudalism. Read **Valley of Seven Castles** to learn more. As of 2016, just 63 billionaires own over half the world's wealth—kings and dukes of a global empire. With nothing to check their power, expect no mercy in the new world odor.

New: YANAPOP

YANAPOP is John Argo's latest high-concept adventure—hopefully to become a series. The initials are a marketing acronym—Young Adult, New Adult, Participating Older Persons (over half the readership of the first two categories consists of older adults trying to escape from dirty books churned out by the desperate gatekeepers of mediocrity in New York City (a publishing industry now virtually entirely foreign-owned, whose books are now mostly produced in Capitalist China).

1996 Internet Publishing Pioneer

Under the **pseudonym John Argo**, he began publishing science fiction and suspense novels online in 1996. He was the first person in history to publish entire (not sample), proprietary (not public domain) novels on the Internet (or Web; not on portable media like CD-ROM or floppies) for reading online in HTML format. These works were offered in a then revolutionary new weekly serial chapter format 1996-1997, with the option to download the entire ms in TXT format. More info at the publisher website; see **Clocktower Books Museum Pages**.

He chose the name John Argo in 1996 while launching his revolutionary new HTML novels online—intending a clear reference to ancient Aegean mythology—the magic ship Argo that transported ancient mariners (Jason and the Argonauts) to mythological and undying adventures.

DarkSF

John Argo's standalone SF novels (and one horror novel, *Doom Spore*) have enough in common to qualify as a series. In fact, the author maintains that most science fiction is inherently dark in nature—meaning it concerns a mythos and cosmos in which human nature and its world are reflections of one another in their terror, imperfection, and ultimately the triumph of right over might (one hopes).

Many of the DarkSF novels are a wonderful trope that the author calls Patina Fiction. See online: www.darksf.com. He has used the same method elsewhere.

New: Patina Fiction

The author often uses a technique he calls Patina Fiction—to reenter the magic shaman space of stories he has enjoyed, and reinvent them in new and original ways. This is what Shakespeare did with Boccaccio, Virgil did with Homer, and contemporary popular author Stephenie Meyer did with *A Midsummer Night's Dream* to create her *Twilight* vampire series. Many authors do it—stand on the shoulders of giants.

For example, **John Argo's DarkSF novel Robinson Crusoe 1,000,000 A.D.** is in the tradition of patina fiction (e.g., the 1964 film *Robinson Crusoe on Mars*) after 1719's archetype written by Daniel Defoe (which has never gone out of print). The original was borrowed from the true story of a shipwrecked Scottish sailor, Alexander Selkirk, who lends his name to John Argo's hero Alex Kirk; while the love interest is Marian Shurey, from Defoe's wife Mary, his mother Annie, and slave Xury who personifies Daniel Defoe's hero's guilt-ridden Calvinist torment; inspiring Crusoe's punishment, including banishment among cannibal horrors.

John Argo's DarkSF novel <u>Monopol City</u> is a cracked mirror reflection of wonder and of terror set in pocket universes that draw on 1930s Golden Age SF, with flavorings of *Brazil* and *The 13th Floor* (1999 dir. Joe Rusnak, starring Gretchen Mol, Vincent D'Onofrio, and Armin Mueller-Stahl among others) and *Inception* (2010 dir. Christopher Nolan, starring Michael Caine, Leonardo DiCaprio, Ellen Page, Tom Berenger, *et al.*) The reason we mention the stellar casts is to underscore the archetypal nature of these stories, and the readiness of top talent to commit to the films.

John Argo's DarkSF novel <u>Nebula Express</u> is a patina fiction reflecting archetypes in Ridley Scott's movie *Alien*—but scarier, because the monsters are both external and internal in Argo's claustrophobic tour de force. *Alien*, which launched a franchise, stars Tom Skerritt, Sigourney Weaver, John Hurt, Ian Holm, and Yaphet Kotto among others. It is worth noting the great casts of these signature films to reflect their patina magnetism.

John Argo's DarkSF novel <u>Streamliners</u> is a patina fiction not of a specific novel or movie, but of genres. It is a thrilling journey among parallel Art Deco worlds, starring the lovers Jeff Maxxon and Lexa Whiston—a powerful tale of history in a blender, a story you must let go to enjoy but your imagination will be dog-walked for you by a master of suspense and vaulting creativity. Reading is believing, whether the story is true or truly a story. The title reflects the culture of the 1920s and 1930s, a strangely creative mix of irrational exuberance and incipient depression between the wars—when King Tut inspired a significant remake of the prewar romanticism of the Art Nouveau era, just as the demagogues and marching decibels of mindless hate and violence would leave the world in ruins by 1945. This novel captures that lost world, and more.

John Argo has promised at least one further fabulous DarkSF novel, already laid out and partially written as of 2016—but under wraps until the big reveal, probably in 2017. It will be an important capstone for the collection.

John Argo's DarkSF novel <u>Doom Spore</u> is a patina fiction reprise of another of the author's favorite films—*Invasion of the Body Snatchers* (1956, dir. Don Siegel, starring Kevin McCarthy, Dana Wynter, and Carolyn Jones). The movie is another archetype that keeps seeing remakes, the original (and John Argo's favorite) being the 1956 version. It is based on the 1955 novel *The Body Snatchers* by Jack Finney (who also wrote one of the all-time great novels combining detective and time travel, titled *Time and Again*, 1970)

John Argo's novel is, again, a totally fresh and original patina fiction spun off from the atmosphere, the aura—the

magic—of these great originals.

John Argo's DarkSF novel <u>This Shoal of Space</u> was released in 1996 online—almost certainly the world's first true e-book published online in HTML format (not on portable media) to be read directly on your computer screen—a complete novel (not partial or sample); proprietary, not public domain (therefore no comparison with the public domain works of Project Gutenberg); standard length (over 120,000 words); and released in a then-innovative format of weekly serial chapters starting in summer 1996. Readers around the world who could not wait to read the end could download a companion TXT file. Still available

today, this novel made history; it also became a bestseller on the first 1999/2000 online retail websites (e.g., NuvoMedia Rocket eBooks, Barnes-Noble).

Empire of Time

Visit the Amazon author pages of <u>John T. Cullen</u>, <u>Jean-Thomas Cullen,</u> and <u>John Argo</u> for more info.

The author has also worked for more than fifty years on a future history—an SF trope that was all the rage back in mid-twentieth century, as pioneered by Isaac Asimov, Robert A. Heinlein, Andre Norton, Alfred Bester, Arthur C. Clarke, and above all, John Argo's pick for the greatest science fiction writer of all time—Cordwainer Smith. Another long-time great was A. E. Van Vogt. And H. P. Lovecraft's science fiction side (e.g., *At The Mountains of Madness*) may be mentioned in this context…but the list quickly grows too long for a complete discussion. Later inheritors of the Future History tradition include movie geniuses like George Lucas (Star Wars), Gene Roddenberry (Star Trek),and more.

The author's first novel, started at age 15 and finished at 19, was *City of the Universe*. It will finally see publication in 2016 after its suppression over fifty years. It is a teenager's novel, yes, but a reasonably good story that should have been published in the 1960s and deserves its airing in the following century.

This "19"—code for *City of the Universe*, or *Cosmopolis*, both titles used by the 1960s for this book—was, and is, the cornerstone of John Argo's future history series. It continues in work today, with various finished works. These include short stories—*Night Songs at Um, City of Mirrors, Harps*—and novels—*Mars the Divine, Lantern Road, Time Train*, Pioneers, *Runners: Escape from Prison Planet or Die*, and recently *Tellerine*.

More Empire of Time Novels…

Of these, the oldest is Pioneers, a novel first written by the author in 1973 at age 23, while the latest is Tellerine, written in 2014. The saga spans eons of time and light years of space, from long before our own Holocene Epoch until the stars in our universe begin to glow dark red and fade at the end of time.

That's just our time, our cosmos, local time. Among infinitely many universes, our cosmos is but a grain of sand—and yet each life is glorious and uproarious.

Joining it all together is the Temporale, a transit world connecting places and times with a rail network launched eons ago by a long lost alien race (LAAR) with a dazzling secret… come, read, and enjoy worlds beyond imagination from the pen of John Argo.

Works by John T. Cullen

Coronado Mystery

The mystery of the Beautiful Stranger is well over a century old now—an 1892 gaslight true crime that became San Diego's most enduring ghost legend. John T. Cullen is the first researcher to propose a plausible solution to the crime, based entirely on true history—which also ties up every loose end in a tangle of mysterious leads covering half of North America.

The author unveils a tragedy—a woman's story—the true manifestation of that Victorian ideal, the Fallen Angel. But this angel was more victim than accomplice. She was single, 24, and pregnant—almost a death sentence in Victorian times. As we learn, it was her second mistake. Misled from her home in Detroit, she became part of an extortion plot at the Hotel del Coronado near San Diego. She was desperate, and willing to do anything for the only two persons in the world she loved—one, her lover, John Longfield, the other a ruthless grifter named Kate Morgan. Their target was the owner of the hotel: John Spreckels, one of the wealthiest men in the Gilded Age.

The plot went horribly wrong, and the Spreckels agents covered admirably for their master—who was at that moment in the White House in Washington, discussing with family friend President Benjamin Harrison the fate of Hawai'i and the Spreckels sugar fortune.

The dead woman was beautiful, elegant young would-be actress Lizzie Wyllie, a poor deluded young shopgirl. These two books bring her memory back to life (more)

(continued: Coronado Mystery)—John T. Cullen, who worked at the Hotel del Coronado part-time while retired, has written two important books about San Diego's most famous legend. The first is **Dead Move: Kate Morgan and the Haunting Mystery of Coronado,** a true nonfictional analysis based on the hotel's official documents plus his own research and knowledge of history. The second (a novel) is **Lethal Journey, a Noir Gaslight Suspense Thriller**. There is nothing supernatural about the story, except the cover (ghost legend) Spreckels' men created to save him from scandal.

Progressive Thrillers

John T. Cullen has long been dedicated to progressive causes including universal healthcare in the United States—the only industrialized nation still living in the dark ages, kept imprisoned behind a vast Berlin Wall of lies and propaganda by the 99% corporate controlled press. They don't want us to understand that they steal up to $1 Trillion per year from our productivity while rapidly bankrupting the country and the middle class as the Reagan-Bush-Cheney disaster careens through its fourth decade of lies, destruction, and meanspiritedness.

CON2: The Generals of October, later **CON2: Autumn of the Republic**

In 1992, the author (a registered Republican "until I woke up" that year) wrote a deliberately nonpartisan warning about a looming Second Constitutional Convention (. He now considers that novel the first of his Progressive Thriller series.

Valley of Seven Castles, a Luxembourg Thriller

The latest progressive thriller hits much harder at the insatiable greed of the 1% who own the United States and the world. In 2016, a global analysis revealed that more than half the world's wealth is owned by just 63 billionaires. These sixty three men are the first of a coming hierarchy of feudal overlords who will soon own the world's land, factories, cities, and people. We will all become serfs and peasants in a horrific new world odor. In Valley of Seven Castles, the oligarchs employ a thin class of skilled workers to do the work of running their global ant farm. This is nothing new.

The ancient Roman republic, on which the USA is modeled, had three classes—the *Patres* (Patricians Fatherly Class) who owned everything and everyone at the beginning of the republic in the sixth century BCE; the *Equites* (Equestrian Class) who were in effect a skilled middle class; and the *Plebs* or *Populus* (People) who were essentially chattels. The Plebeians fought for centuries to gain civil rights—only to lose everything in the chaos in the twilight of the republic in the age of Cicero, Pompey, Caesar, Mark Antony, Cleopatra, and other players in the final century before Augustus (Octavian) created a 500-year tyranny (empire)—with the complicity of wealthy oligarchs: both old money (*Boni, Optimates*) and new money (*Novi, Populares*). From there on, it was all bread and games of the circus until the lights went out at the dawn of feudal Europe: history repeating itself?

(continued: Progressive Thrillers)—

Valley of Seven Castles is a thriller with a deep secret—it is based on the plot structure of several successive super-thrillers in history. The first of these is the 1915 British spy thriller The Thirty-Nine Steps by John Buchan. Its ten chapter plot pattern was adapted into film in 1935 by Alfred Hitchcock. As the author reveals on the webside www.progressivethriller.com and in the About sections at the back of the book, Alfred Hitchcock had yet another trick up his sleeve—North by Northwest, another of the world's most famous thriller films. Once you understand the plot features, you'll see why the three stories (and now a fourth, Valley of Seven Castles) belong to a unique group of stories carved from the same tree.

The hero and heroine of Valley of Seven Castles are on the run for their lives across Europe—much like the characters played by Matt Damon and Franka Potente in The Bourne Identity. Rick Buchan is a U.S. Army deserter wanted for a crime he didn't commit. Hannah Smith, a California girl, is a contractual slave—a BAN—who has escaped from her Chinese billionaire owner, and she's taken a powerful military secret with her that has thugs all over Europe hunting for her. Together with Rick, she will get the IFS (Intelligent Fuselage Skin) into the hands of PAX, a progressive world front that combats the growing rule of the tyrants like Wan, Hannah's owner. What's fact and what's fiction? You decide as you enjoy this riveting story.

(continued: Progressive Thrillers)—CON2: Autumn of the Republic (originally *The Generals of October*) is a rousing suspense story with a powerful and scary warning about our future. Upon endless calls to invoke Article V—a ticking time bomb in the U.S. Constitution—a convention of state delegations is called in Washington under the most massive military presence since the Civil War. And the result is—civil war. Like all of John T. Cullen's novels, there is a tender, engaging love story as young army officers Captain David Gordon and Lt. Victoria 'Tory' Breen hunt the mysterious murderer of a Coast Guard computer specialist and end up uncovering a plot by traitorous generals, slimy corporate politicians, and other dark forces to throw out the 1787 U.S. Constitution and replace it with a new 'biblical' document that will make corporate CEOs salivate with joy at their new limitless power. Every dog gets a bone in this junkyard—unless Tory and David can expose the plot of the Generals of October and save the nation with the help of sympathetic patriots who have their heads screwed on right and understand the need for human rights and an enlightened understanding of what the Framing Fathers of 1787 intended—not what corrupt politicians, generals, religious zealots, and false news hacks prefer.

Doctor Night, a *Tomorrow Thriller* by John T. Cullen

In this riveting near-future thriller, Jack Gray is the agent of last resort in a world ruled by competing corporations. Like James Bond's Kremlin (Smersh), Jack Gray fights for a corporate empire including the formerly sovereign U.S. against an implacable adversary right out of Ian Fleming's playbook. Now a new force raises its head (Spectre, anyone?), far more terrifying: a global terror brokerage (Black Umbrella). It's been taken over by a megalomaniac who calls himself Doctor Night. Jack Gray must save the world when Doctor Night captures a satellite technology (OST) that permits his private forces to assassinate world leaders from outer space. Based on 1950s technology run amok, it's plausible—and will probably soon be announced by world governments.

Two Totally Different Novels

The Christmas Clock

RAY BRADBURY in January 2008 sent John T. Cullen a personal note, praising *The Christmas Clock*. Scribbled on an envelope (not our first correspondence), an ailing Ray wrote: "Bravo, John! Read and loved your Clock." It's a dark holiday fantasy with several unforgettable features: a crotchety old banker who plays the modern version of Charles Dickens' Scrooge; a harried genie out of a Middle Eastern bottle, in the form of a young executive who is constantly talking on his cell phone with his superiors somewhere in the clouds; and Time's River of Dust, on which the fate of all people and all things passes through channels of circumstance. It's a novel with special significance for those whose lives and loves have been hurt by alcoholism.

The Spy's Daughter

(originally titled *Umnitsa, The Clever Girl*) is a long, moving symphony of espionage, war, love, betrayal, and redemption spanning half a century, three continents, and many lives. Its passion will remind you of *Doctor Zhivago*, the novel by Boris Pasternak (not the shmaltz movie starring Julie Christie and Omar Sharif) except the tale is told more clearly and sharply. The scope will remind readers of Herman Wouk's panoramic novels, and the author likes to think of John Dos Passos' *USA Trilogy* as a background model.

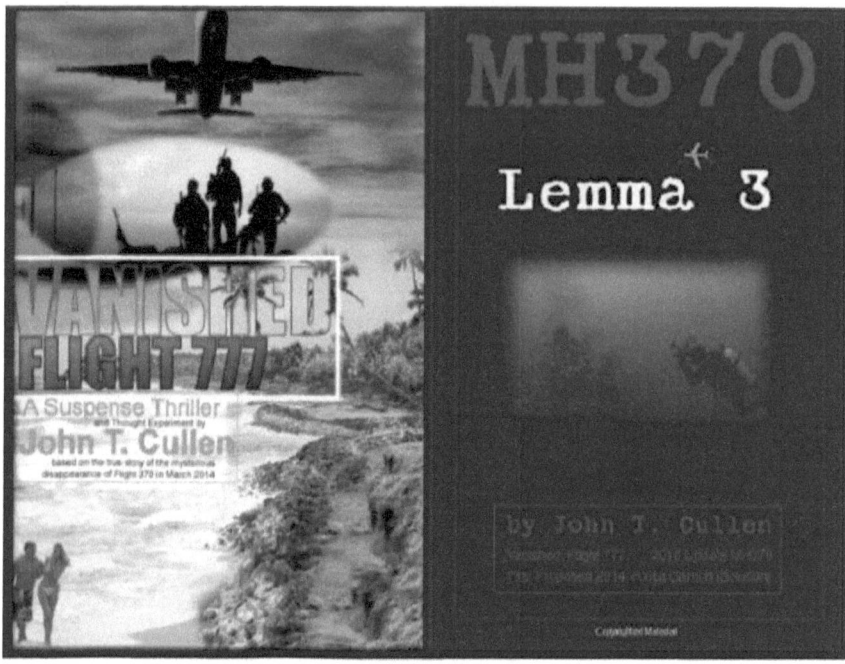

Vanished Flight MH370 and sequel Lemma 3

When Malaysian Airlines Flight MH370 vanished without a trace on the night of 8 March 2014, John T. Cullen—ever an avid researcher and investigator—began to see a pattern. He closely followed the breaking news, and researched the history of the region, and developed a stunningly plausible theory. He wrote a Tomorrow Thriller starring Jack Dorsey and his team of commandos, who are diverted from an R&R vacation on a tropical island to aid in the investigation of a fictional mystery quite like the real one. The missing flight in the novel is Flight 777, named after the Boeing model (777-200ER) to avoid confusing readers amid all the conspiracy books that inevitably cropped up like mushrooms after rain.

Two years later, on the anniversary date of 8 March 2016, it was established that Flight MH370 had crashed into the Indian Ocean. The official version, buttressed by questionable officials in the region, is that the plane went down off the eastern coast of Australia. Tidal drift charts for the Indian Ocean do not contradict the fact that parts began turning up on the coasts of Africa. Nor do the same charts differ in John T. Cullen's theory that MH370 was hijacked by terrorists. In Lemma 3, the terrifying third and most plausible explanation, the crime was committed by enemies of the West and of modern civilization (Al Qaeda, ISIL, or maybe some suspect governments in the region?). Their intent was to take the plane to Africa (hello?) and weaponize it, after which they would drop it on a propaganda target more valuable than New York City and the Pentagon on 9/11. The author has further theorized that the plane (seen by reliable witnesses on Maldives, a claim denied by chaotic and suspect officials) was in trouble and going down in the early morning hours of 8 March 2014. It went into the Indian Ocean west of Maldives, on a bearing for the Horn of Africa. Its wings sheared off, which is why it is wing debris washing up off Africa—while the fuselage rests intact on the abyssal Arabian Basin or in the underwater mountain ranges.

The author published his first novel, labeled "a novel and thought experiment," in early June 2014. With wing debris washing up around Africa, he felt compelled to issue a second edition—Lemma 3, the third and most terrifying option (hijack with malicious intent). The mission failed—but we must study the possibilities to avoid becoming victims of yet another major terrorist attack like 9/11.

Note: Lemma 3 contains the same text and maps as Vanished Flight 777. Both editions now have a lengthy prolog as an update. Read either edition—they are the same except for the gripping cover images.

Works by Jean-Thomas Cullen

Jean-Thomas Cullen (author's actual birth name) always writes novels with a strong female lead and a strong male lead. Each is a powerful love story because it strongly undergirds the main story. Except for Lethal Journey, there is always HEA (Happy Ever After). This is not category romance by definition, since the love story is not the primary plot. In one instance, the author decided to experiment. He wrote a love story that is the primary plot. Stop By: The Millionaire and the Librarian fits into the 'clean' category—no explicit sex, and no gratuitous violence. It's simply a very powerful love story about Rick Meyer, 31, a millionaire on the rebound from a bitter divorce, and Marian 'the Librarian' Charles, a beautiful twenty-something war widow. Reading is believing— women readers have described it as a 'wonderful, sweet little love story.'

The author was a young soldier stationed in West Germany 1975-1980 when he wrote this tender, melancholy novel about a passionate love affair. It was pure nostalgia, written in an old Hitler-era barracks nights while moths and ghosts danced about and Mozart played softly at his side. He was having a blast, traveling around Europe in an old orange VW van with his friends. Like most G.I.s far from home, he was lonely for 'the World' as the U.S. is called. So he wrote this retrospective fiction about a young poet (23) and a beautiful, neglected young faculty wife in a New England college town. The story is surprisingly powerful and sophisticated, coming from a young author. Cryptically titled Jon+Merile, the manuscript gathered dust for 40 years until now. At the same time, the author had finished his

CLOCKTOWER BOOKS, SAN DIEGO

life as a lyric poet at age 27—the mythological year of burnout for rock stars and other poets. Unlike Jim Morrison, Jimi Hendrix, Janis Joplin, Kurt Cobain, and Amy Winehouse to name a few, he did not die. He flamed out as a poet and turned his energies to writing novels like *The Spy's Daughter*, *This Shoal of Space*, or *Tellerine*, which are all poetic love stories. In 2016, we publish the author's "27"—the novel (*On Saint Ronan Street*), the poems (*Cymbalist Poems*), and then both together in one volume—*27duet*. Some readers may only want to read the poems, others only the love story (with selected poems inserted), and others will want to enjoy the two together—twins separated a birth, reunited years later.

Insets: from the cover of 27duet, left; Cymbalist Poems, right.

A Walk in Ancient Rome

John T. Cullen is an avid researcher and history/science writer. Among his articles and stories, the magnum opus is his *A Walk in Ancient Rome*. Well received by experts on ancient Roman history and topology in galleys, the book will see its first authorized release in 2016. It is a virtual tour of the ancient capital *ca* 330 in the age of Constantine—a walk through each of the fourteen imperial districts with lively and informed *cicerone* talk as if we are really there—hearing crowds, smelling fresh bread, incense, an intense mix of other sights and sounds. The author has done his homework (Platner, Ashby, Richards, Beard, Carcopino, and many more) and knows how to narrate history at each corner.

The author has published, or is publishing, articles on other topics in The Reading Room at Clocktower Books. All titles available at Amazon. Topics and inquiries in the nonfiction series include: Homer, Nostradamus, the Sator Enigma, climate change, Hitler, and much more—even how to bake a tasty pizza in 22 minutes at home.

John T. Cullen (B.A., B.B.A., M.S.B.A.), a trained researcher, keeps his writing at a standard acceptable to subject matter experts. He has a rigorous understanding of research and an academic's respect for a subject. He is an independent scholar who clearly explains when there may be several answers to a question (as frequently happens; e.g., the Archaic Triad on the Quirinal Hill in ancient Rome) and he clearly states when a statement is his own opinion. His goal is to entertain and to edify, not to mislead or confuse.

A readily available example of his scholarship is *Dead Move: Kate Morgan and the Haunting Mystery of Coronado* (over 120 footnotes). This is a work of nonfiction, closely researched, full of identified sources. It is also a ground-breaking analysis that finally solves the enigma of the Beautiful Stranger. Most remarkable is the fact that the answers have been hidden in plain sight all along. You only have to study the facts of known history for it all to make sense. This is the philosophy he applies in his nonfiction series SHIPS—Secrets Hidden In Plain Sight—includes articles on Nostradamus, Homer, the Sator Enigma, and more.

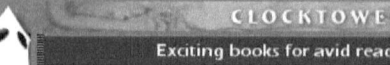
About Clocktower Books

Clocktower Books, a pioneering e-book and Print on Demand publisher, launched in April 1996 by publishing the world's first entire (not partial) proprietary (not public domain) novels (long works, industry standard) for reading online in HTML format (not for reading on portable media like CD-ROM, floppies, or other intermediary media).

We have been an omnibus publisher (e-book and print) since 1996.

We are honored to have on board such excellent authors as Dr. Renée B. Horowitz, Ph.D. (author of the Rx Pharmacy Sleuth Trilogy and other novels), Dennis Latham (The Bad Season, etc.), Robin Marchesi (A Small Journal of Heroin Addiction), and other fine talent.

The publisher, Jean-Thomas Cullen, continues to release novels and shorter fiction, as well as books and articles of nonfiction—primarily on history, but also on science and other topics. His pseudonyms of choice include Jean-Thomas Cullen (his real birth name), John T. Cullen, and John Argo.

To learn about our latest offerings, please visit the website at

www.clocktowerbooks.com

You will find at the Museum Pages on our website a detailed history of our pioneering publishing house starting from 1996—including references and documentation (ever a work in progress).

From 1998 to 2007, Clocktower Books also published what was, during its run, the world's first professional Web-only (online) magazine of speculative and dark fiction (or SFFH). We published new authors as well as officers and top names of the Science Fiction Writers of America (SFWA); more on our pioneering work at the Science Fiction Encyclopedia online (look under Far Sector).

Our magazine's major names over the years included **Deep Outside SFFH** and **Far Sector SFFH**. We published many nominees or later awardees of the Hugo, Nebula, Sturgeon, and other global awards including British, Canadian, and Australian. The leading SF magazine historian Mike Ashley (Liverpool University Press) has stated he will recognize our pioneering magazine in the final final volume of his authoritative SF magazine histories.

More Works by this Author

For upcoming books and articles by the author, check oneline at www.johntcullen.com or www.clocktowerbooks.com among other sites.

www.ingramcontent.com/pod-product-compliance
Lightning Source LLC
Chambersburg PA
CBHW022031170626
46808CB00003B/1142